Mayors
Community Workers

by Alice K. Flanagan

Content Adviser: Joan Crigger,
U.S. Conference of Mayors

Reading Adviser: Dr. Linda D. Labbo,
College of Education, Department of Reading Education,
The University of Georgia

COMPASS POINT BOOKS

Minneapolis, Minnesota

Compass Point Books
3109 West 50th Street, #115
Minneapolis, MN 55410

Visit Compass Point Books on the Internet at *www.compasspointbooks.com* or e-mail your
request to *custserv@compasspointbooks.com*

Photographs ©:
Gregg Andersen, cover; J. Taposchaner/FPG International, 4; Unicorn Stock Photos/David Cummings, 5; Richard
Laird/FPG International, 6; Reuters/Mike Segar/Archive Photos, 7; Unicorn Stock Photos/Dick Young, 8; Charles
Gupton/Pictor, 9; Unicorn Stock Photos/Tom McCarthy, 10; Reuters/Lou Dematteis/Archive Photos, 11; John Terence
Turner/FPG International, 12; Reuters/Fred Prouser/Archive Photos, 13; Daemmrich/Pictor, 14; AFP/Corbis, 15;
Reuters/William Philpott/Archive Photos, 16; Unicorn Stock Photos/Chris Boylan, 17; Reuters/Brad Rickerby/Archive
Photos, 18; Unicorn Stock Photos/Arni Katz, 19; Photo Network/Bachmann, 20; Reuters NewMedia Inc./Corbis, 21;
Jim Mejuto/FPG International, 24; Arthur Tilley/FPG International, 24, 25; Reuters/Scott Olson/Archive Photos, 26;
Charles Gupton/Pictor, 27.

Editors: E. Russell Primm and Emily J. Dolbear
Photo Researcher: Svetlana Zhurkina
Photo Selector: Linda S. Koutris
Designer: Bradfordesign, Inc.

Library of Congress Cataloging-in-Publication Data

Flanagan, Alice K.
    Mayors / by Alice K. Flanagan.
       p. cm. — (Community workers)
    Includes bibliographical references (p.) and index.
    Summary: Introduces the work of running a city, including duties, training, skills needed, and
contribution to the community.
    ISBN 0-7565-0064-8 (lib. bdg.)
    1. Mayors—Juvenile literature. 2. Mayors—Vocational guidance—Juvenile literature. [1. Mayors.
2. Occupations.] I. Title.
    II. Series.
    JS141 .F53 2001
    352.23'216'02373—dc   2100-011718

Table of Contents

WE
RECYCLE

What Do Mayors Do?

A **mayor** makes sure your city or town runs well. He or she works to improve life for the city's **citizens**. A mayor spends the city's money on **public services**. Police and fire departments and parks are public services. Public buses, hospitals, and schools are public services too.

Mayors make sure that cities and towns stay clean.

Mayors oversee the city's fire department.

Where Do They Work?

Mayors work in an office. They work in a building called **city hall**. Mayors often travel around the city. They visit neighbor-hoods and go to meetings. They speak in front of cameras and reporters. Mayors also go to the scene of emergencies after large storms or fires.

◀ Mayors work in city halls.

A mayor on the go speaks to reporters. ▶

Who Do Mayors Work With?

Mayors hire people to help them. These people are called their **staff**. Mayors also work with neighborhood leaders called **councilpersons**. These leaders and the mayor make up the **city council**. Mayors also work with their state's governor.

◀ A mayor works closely with his staff.

A mayor meets ▶ with her city council.

Mayors work with the bosses of the city workers. City workers protect the city's citizens, teach school, and work in libraries. City workers also fix roads, drive buses, and collect garbage. Mayors also work with community leaders.

◄ A town's mayor often meets with the bosses of city workers.

Sometimes ► mayors march with community groups.

What Training Does It Take?

There are no requirements to be a mayor. A person just has to win the most votes in the election. Many mayors have college degrees, however. Some are lawyers. Other have run their own businesses. Some have worked in other areas of government.

Working in a business and dealing with the public is good training to be a mayor.

Mayors should be good public speakers.

What Skills Do They Need?

Mayors are leaders. They must know how to get people to work with them. They should know how to take charge and make decisions. They have to be calm in times of emergencies.

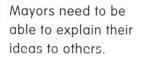
Mayors need to be able to explain their ideas to others.

Mayors have to lead during emergencies. ▶

Mayors need to speak and write well. They give many speeches. They answer questions from the press. Mayors also make a **budget** for the city. So, they have to be able to work with money and numbers.

A mayor speaks to the public.

A mayor visits the site of a new library.

What Tools and Equipment Do They Use?

Mayors need to stay in touch. That's why they use the telephone so much. Mayors also need to know the latest news. They read books, newspapers, and magazines. They use television, radio, and computers to help them get their job done.

Mayors communicate with the public on television and radio.

Mayors use the telephone to stay in touch.

What Problems Do They Face?

Mayors work long hours. They make tough decisions. They have to decide how to spend the city's budget. They have to decide whether to repair streets or hire more teachers. Mayors cannot please everyone. Also, mayors have to win elections to keep their jobs.

◀ Mayors make sure that schools have enough teachers.

A mayor votes ▶ in his own election.

How Do Mayors Help?

Cities and towns would not run smoothly without mayors. Mayors make sure public services are there for everyone. They make sure public libraries, schools, parks, and hospitals are open to all citizens. And they keep the city safe.

◀ Keeping public buildings open and safe is one of a mayor's many jobs.

Mayors make ▶ sure the roads are clear during snowstorms.

Would You Like to Be a Mayor?

Do you like working with people? Do you like to be in charge? Maybe you would like to be a mayor someday. You can prepare now. At home, help your parents make grocery lists, pay bills, and do jobs around the house. In school, be a leader. Be someone who takes charge.

◀ You can learn to be a leader at an early age.

Being responsible at home is good practice for being a leader. ▶

A Mayor's Tools and Clothes

newspaper camera

suit

microphone

TV camera

Meeting with the Mayor

plan for new neighborhood

reporter

citizen

councilperson

mayor

councilperson's notes

mayor's notes

builder

builder's notes

A Mayor's Day

Morning

- A mayor goes to a breakfast meeting with her staff.
- She and her assistant discuss her plans for the day.
- She goes to the opening of a new library in her city.
- The mayor meets with other city leaders to talk about next year's budget.

Noon

- The mayor speaks at a lunch honoring the state governor.
- Later, she talks to the governor about problems in her city.

Afternoon

- The mayor meets with a local group of fire fighters.
- She holds a meeting with reporters about building new schools in the city.
- The mayor greets a group of Boy Scouts who are visiting city hall that day.

Evening

- Before leaving city hall, she meets with her staff again to prepare for the next day.
- She has dinner with a software-company president who wants to bring business to her city.
- She returns home to watch the evening news.

Glossary

budget—a plan for collecting and spending money

citizens—people who live in a town or city

city council—the city government group that makes and carries out laws

city hall—the main building of a local government

councilpersons—members of a city council

mayor—the head of a local government

public services—things provided by the government for all citizens, such as education, snow removal, and roads

staff—a group of workers

Did You Know?

- From the smallest towns to the largest cities, the United States has thousands of mayors.

- La Guardia Airport in New York City is named for the city's mayor from 1934 to 1945—Fiorello La Guardia.

- In Austria and Germany, the mayor is often called the burgomaster.

- Actor-director Clint Eastwood was the mayor of Carmel, California, from 1986 to 1988.

Want to Know More?

At the Library

Burby, Liza N. *A Day in the Life of a Mayor: Featuring New York Mayor Rudy Giuliani*. New York: PowerKids Press, 1999.

Martinez, Elizabeth Coonrod. *Henry Cisneros: Mexican American Leader*. Brookfield, Conn.: Millbrook, 1994.

On the Web

For more information on mayors, use FactHound to track down Web sites related to this book.

1. Go to *www.facthound.com*
2. Type in a search word related to this book or this book ID: 0756500648
3. Click on the *Fetch It* button.

Your trusty FactHound will fetch the best Web sites for you!

Through the Mail

The U.S. Conference of Mayors

1620 I Street, N.W.
Washington, DC 20006
To get information about mayors in the United States

On the Road

Old City Hall

Fifth and Chestnut Streets
Philadelphia, PA 19106
215/597-8974
To get a historical look at city government

Index

About the Author
Alice K. Flanagan writes books for children and teachers.
Since she was a young girl, she has enjoyed writing. She has
written more than seventy books on a wide variety of topics.
Some of her books include biographies of U.S. presidents
and their wives, biographies of people working in our
neighborhoods, phonics books for beginning readers,
and informational books about birds and Native Americans.
Alice K. Flanagan lives in Chicago, Illinois.